T0368617

Mark 10:14

*A Devotional of Comfort and Hope
for Those Suffering from Miscarriage,
Stillbirth, or Infant Loss*

Crystal Wagner

WestBow Press books may be ordered through booksellers or by contacting:

WestBow Press
A Division of Thomas Nelson & Zondervan
1663 Liberty Drive
Bloomington, IN 47403
www.westbowpress.com
844-714-3454

Because of the dynamic nature of the Internet, any web addresses or links contained in this book may have changed since publication and may no longer be valid. The views expressed in this work are solely those of the author and do not necessarily reflect the views of the publisher, and the publisher hereby disclaims any responsibility for them.

Any people depicted in stock imagery provided by Getty Images are models, and such images are being used for illustrative purposes only.
Certain stock imagery © Getty Images.

• All Scripture quotations are taken from the Holy Bible, NEW INTERNATIONAL VERSION®, NIV® Copyright © 1973, 1978, 1984, 2011 by Biblica, Inc.® Used by permission. All rights reserved worldwide.

ISBN: 979-8-3850-3974-6 (sc)
ISBN: 979-8-3850-3975-3 (hc)
ISBN: 979-8-3850-4115-2 (e)

Library of Congress Control Number: 2024927127

Print information available on the last page.

WestBow Press rev. date: 12/20/2024

WESTBOW
P R E S S®
A DIVISION OF THOMAS NELSON
& ZONDERVAN

Contents

Preface

Our baby was due to be born on October 20, 2011. We were very excited for his arrival, although we didn't know the gender until he was born. It took us close to two years to conceive Blake, and it seemed that our prayers were answered. On the evening of October 15, my water broke. We made our way to the hospital expecting a normal delivery. We were so excited that our baby was ready to make his or her arrival.

The nurses quickly made preparations but struggled to find a heartbeat. After some trying, the nurse looked me in the eye and said, "I am so sorry." We continued to have hope that she was wrong and patiently waited for my doctor to arrive. When she did, she quickly performed an ultrasound. Our fears were confirmed as she searched for a heartbeat. Nothing. Our baby was gone.

On October 16, 2011, at 5:30 a.m., Blake Joseph Wagner was born. The room was silent as they took my baby away from the room. There was no sound other than the footsteps of the doctor who carried him. The nurses asked if we wanted some time to hold him. They brought him back for us to hold and say our goodbyes. Blake was perfect in every way. Shawn and I held him at the hospital as long as we could. We left the hospital the next day empty. Empty in every sense of the word.

In the days and years following, we drew closer to God. Through His word, he speaks to mothers and families who have experienced this loss. I have captured a few of these Bible verses and what I have learned through this experience. We hope you find comfort in this book and the scriptures contained within.

Until we meet again.

My baby is in heaven.

For any mother who has experienced miscarriage, stillbirth, or infant or child loss, we take comfort in knowing that our babies are in heaven with Jesus. When Jesus walked on this earth, people brought their children to Jesus so that He would bless them. He welcomed them into His arms. Jesus loves children. It is quite possible the first thing our babies saw as they entered heaven was the face of Jesus.

He said to them, "Let the little children come to me, and do not hinder them, for the kingdom of God belongs to such as these."

—Mark 10:14 (NIV)

My baby had an angelic escort to paradise.

Have you ever thought about how one's soul leaves this earth and enters heaven? In the parable of the rich man and Lazarus, the Bible tells us that angels carried Lazarus to Abraham's side to be comforted. This story told by Jesus gives us insight into the way our babies entered paradise, in the arms of angels.

The time came when the beggar died and the angels carried him to Abraham's side. The rich man also died and was buried.

—Luke 16:22 (NIV)

Heaven is the ultimate goal.

As parents, we want our children to be healthy and happy, but selfishly, we want them with us as long as we live. It is a parent's hope that their children outlive them and raise their own family. As God's children, our desire is to be in heaven with our Father. In heaven, we will have eternal peace and joy with immortal bodies that never grow old. Our goal is not how many years we live, how much money we have, or what car we drive. Our babies made the ultimate goal, which is to be with our maker: our Lord and Savior.

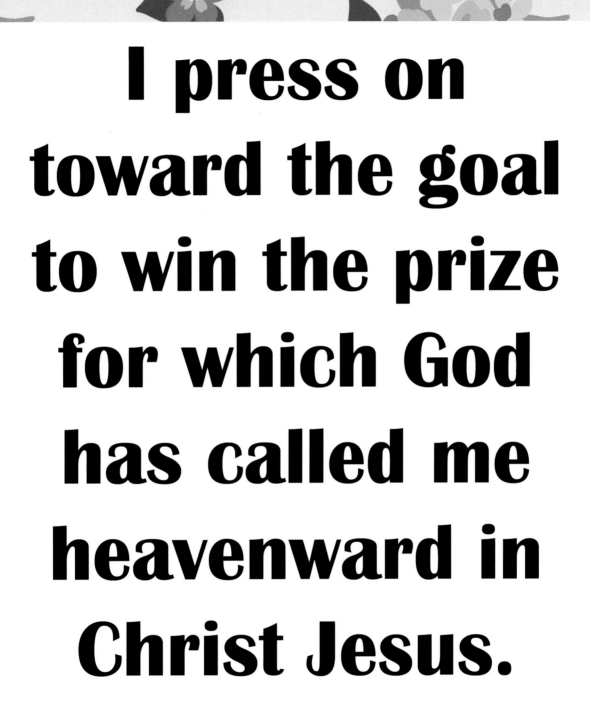

I press on toward the goal to win the prize for which God has called me heavenward in Christ Jesus.

—Philippians 3:14 (NIV)

My baby was perfect.

When a baby passes, we want to know why. Our minds want to reason why a baby is gone too soon.

Our babies were perfect in every way. Please do not let anyone tell you differently. There may be a medical reason to explain the early passing of a child, but God has His perfect way in everything and everyone—regardless of the size of our footprints.

The book of Psalms tells us that God meticulously pieced us together while in our mother's womb. The word used by David is translated as "knit." Do you know someone who knits? Loops of yarn are made to interlace with other loops to make beautiful pieces of art, blankets, and hats. We are wonderfully made by Him who made the earth and all the wonders in it as well as the skies.

For you created my inmost being; you knit me together in my mother's womb. I praise you because I am fearfully and wonderfully made; your works are wonderful, I know that full well.

—Psalm 139:1-14 (NIV)

I cannot bring my baby back.

When the nurse told us that there was no heartbeat, I held out hope that she was wrong. I prayed that she made a mistake. It was not until the doctor arrived to do an ultrasound and I could see no flutter or movement that I began to believe it to be true. But still I continued to pray. Maybe God would spare me the grief and the pain. Perhaps God would give my child to me if I held on to that hope.

After my baby was born and the doctor took him from the room, I felt empty and ashamed. It was quiet as the nurses tended to my body, which was numb in every sense of the word. It was not until the funeral service for Blake that I fully understood this passage from 2 Samuel and David's words to his servants.

We cannot bring our babies back, but we can go to them through a relationship with Jesus Christ.

He answered, "While the child was still alive, I fasted and wept. I thought, 'Who knows? The Lord may be gracious to me and let the child live.' But now that he is dead, why should I go on fasting? Can I bring him back again? I will go to him, but he will not return to me."

—2 Samuel 12:2-23 (NIV)

God does not make mistakes.

God knew my baby before he was conceived. He knew me before I was conceived.

My baby was set apart for a purpose. God's purpose. Our purpose in all we do is to glorify God.

God has specific plans for our lives no matter how brief. As it is said, sometimes the smallest footprints leave the biggest impressions.

Before I formed you in the womb I knew you, before you were born I set you apart; I appointed you as a prophet to the nations.

—Jeremiah 1:5 (NIV)

There is no pain or tears in heaven.

Can you imagine a place with no pain or tears because there is no sickness or death? A place where this is no need for doctors, hospitals, or medicine. Jesus defeated death. He is our redeemer and the great physician.

I simply cannot imagine the joy we will feel and the peace that will fill our hearts as we forever worship Him with all who have gone on before us.

He will wipe every tear from their eyes. There will be no more death or mourning or crying or pain, for the old order of things has passed away.

—Revelation 21:4 (NIV)

There is no darkness in heaven.

A common fear among humans is darkness. When it is dark, our sight is restricted and other senses step in, making us hear things that we would not typically hear. Or we may see things in the shadows. To me, a storm is scarier at night when the sky cannot be seen.

In heaven there is no darkness. There is no need for a night light or the light of the sun for God gives light and the Lamb is the lamp.

There will be no more night. They will not need the light of a lamp or the light of the sun, for the Lord God will give them light. And they will reign for ever and ever.

—Revelation 22:5 (NIV)

God will use this for good.

Romans 8:28 is one of my favorite Bible verses. There is a reason for everything. He is in control—not me. I knew there was a reason that Blake was born sleeping, but I could not see in the days following his stillbirth the plans God had in store for our lives.

On the night we lost Blake, I swore that our firstborn daughter would be an only child. On the one-year anniversary of Blake's funeral service, the Lord blessed us with twins. We were blessed two years later with another baby girl. I cannot imagine our life without them. We remember Blake and miss him dearly, but his death will not be in vain. Our mission as a family is to help others who have experienced this loss.

God will use your loss for good too. God is drawing you nearer to Him. He wants you to lean into His love and comfort to give you understanding and peace. You will feel His word calling you with an unquenchable thirst for knowledge of His divine plan. In this, your faith will strengthen.

And we know that in all things God works for the good of those who love him, who have been called according to his purpose.

–Romans 8:28 (NIV)

Do not let the devil steal your joy.

The devil is going to tell you that it was your fault. You will replay everything you did in the weeks and days prior to losing your baby. He will put thoughts into your head to make you question your worth or your ability to care for a baby. Then he will want you to separate from your friends, family, and church. He wants you to feel alone like you are the only woman who failed to raise a child.

It is OK to be sad. Perhaps now is your time to grieve, but you will see your baby again. Remember the moments you were blessed with, even if only for a little while. Do not let anyone take away your joy.

So with you: Now is your time of grief, but I will see you again and you will rejoice, and no one will take away your joy.

—John 16:22 (NIV)

Be Strong and Courageous

Losing a baby is traumatic. Where there were life and hope for a future, emptiness and shame move in, making even getting out of bed dreadful—let alone facing family and friends. After some time and healing, you may want to try to conceive again. Worry and anxiety try to take residence in your mind, but you must overcome them. This will take strength and courage from above, placing all your trust and faith in God to carry you through.

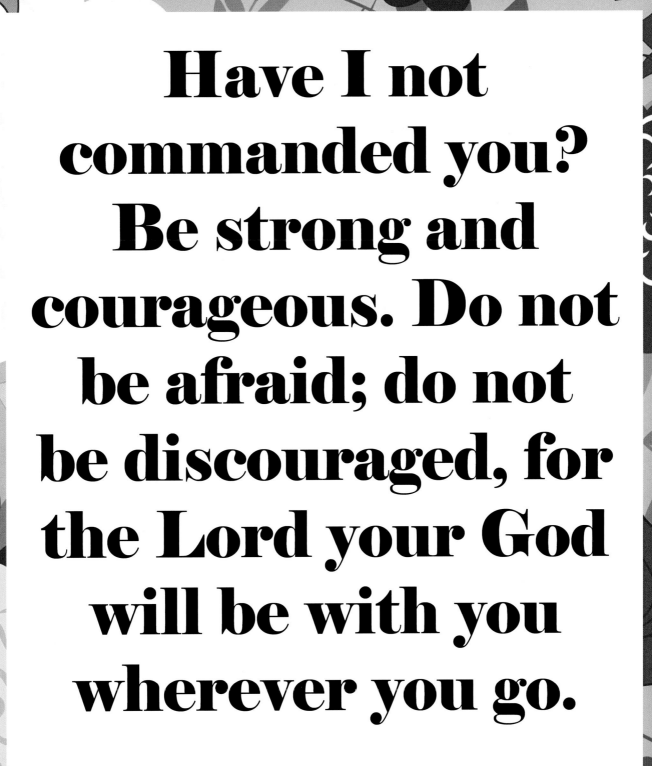

Have I not commanded you? Be strong and courageous. Do not be afraid; do not be discouraged, for the Lord your God will be with you wherever you go.

—Joshua 1:9 (NIV)

It is OK to grieve.

It is OK to mourn the loss of your baby. Even Jesus cried when His friend Lazarus died. Lazarus had two sisters, Mary, and Martha. They were distraught at the loss of their brother. In the shortest verse in the English language, the Bible tells us that "Jesus wept." He knew that He was going to raise Lazarus and that Lazarus would live again with the command of His voice, but Jesus grieved because His friends were hurting.

We know that our babies are in heaven and that we will see them again, yet we grieve and mourn our loss. Even years later, we are saddened, but we have the hope of eternity with them again.

Jesus wept.

—John 11:35 (NIV)

It is not your fault.

When a mother's womb empties after a miscarriage or a stillbirth, a feeling of shame with guilt becomes overwhelming and a mother often questions, "What did I do to deserve this?"

We all fall short of the glory of God daily, but listen to me when I tell you God is not trying to punish you. Yes, He wants you to draw closer to Him, but your baby's loss is not a penalty for sin. Jesus died for our sins as the perfect sacrifice.

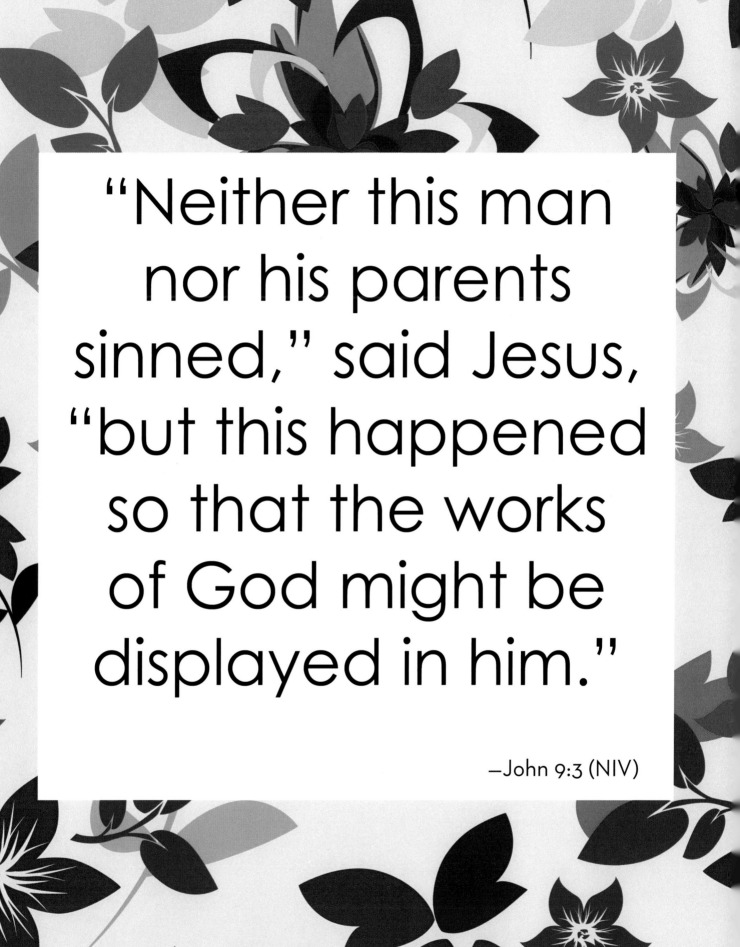

"Neither this man nor his parents sinned," said Jesus, "but this happened so that the works of God might be displayed in him."

—John 9:3 (NIV)

Heaven is beautiful.

We cannot even begin to imagine the beauty of heaven and all its splendor. Not only are the streets made of gold and the river of life flowing through it is as clear as crystal, but our Father is there with Jesus and all the saints. Jesus left this earth to prepare a place for those who love him. Our babies are there waiting for the sweet day when we are reunited together—forever.

However, as it is written:"What no eye has seen, what no ear has heard, and what no human mind has conceived"— the things God has prepared for those who love him.

–1 Corinthians 2:9 (NIV)

The Lord gives, and He takes away.

The Lord blessed us with our firstborn daughter rather quickly. When we were ready to add another child to our family, it took much longer. We were faced with infertility as many couples are. We prayed, and once we had all but given up on having any more children, we became pregnant with Blake. It was the perfect pregnancy, but just four days short of our due date, Blake was born sleeping.

A few short months later, we were blessed with another pregnancy—with not one but two babies. When I told my dad that we were expecting twins, he reminded me of the story of Job. The Lord gives, and He takes away. He took one away and gave me two more.

Naked I came from my mother's womb, and naked I will depart. The Lord gave and the Lord has taken away; may the name of the Lord be praised.

—Job 1:21 (NIV)

The Lord will give you strength.

In that time of shame, emptiness, and profound grief, the Lord will hold you up and give you strength. He will give you the words to say to share your story and help educate and edify others. He will never leave you. We were created to worship and glorify Him. All glory to His name!

But the Lord stood at my side and gave me strength, so that through me the message might be fully proclaimed and all the Gentiles might hear it. And I was delivered from the lion's mouth.

—2 Timothy 4:17 (NIV)

We were created for a purpose.

I was created for a purpose. My baby was created for His purpose. Everyone has a story, but God is not finished writing yours. Trust in Him and glorify Him in all that you do. God is still writing my story. He is not done with me yet.

"For I know the plans I have for you," declares the Lord, "plans to prosper you and not to harm you, plans to give you hope and a future."

—Jeremiah 29:11 (NIV)

Our babies never endured the pain of this world.

The world is full of pain and wrongdoing. The evil one rules this world.

After I lost Blake, I was reminded that Blake never had to endure the pain of this world. My heart pondered on this for days after hearing this truth. Babies who pass in the womb were never hungry, cold, alone, afraid, or deceived. Blake only knew the love we had for him.

Your baby felt the love you have and will forever hold a special place in your heart.

While evildoers and impostors will go from bad to worse, deceiving and being deceived.

—2 Timothy 3:13 (NIV)

Jesus overcame the world.

As painful as this world is—full of misery and sorrow—Jesus reminds us in the book of John to take heart for He overcame the world and the evil one. Jesus defeated death to give us eternal life.

I have told you these things, so that in me you may have peace. In this world you will have trouble. But take heart! I have overcome the world.

—John 16:33 (NIV)

God does not waste pain.

After losing Blake, I wanted to know why. I asked, "What plans does God have?" I knew there was a purpose in all of it, but I wanted so badly to see it right away. God uses our pain and suffering. We may never fully understand why, but we know God never wastes pain.

Not only so, but we also glory in our sufferings, because we know that suffering produces perseverance; perseverance, character; and character, hope.

—Romans 5:3-4 (NIV)

Have compassion and comfort others.

We are to help others and share the good news with all. Not only are we commissioned to do so, but God also commands us to comfort others as we have been comforted. As parents with babies who left to be with the Lord, we are to comfort other parents facing the same circumstances. As Esther was told, perhaps you were born for a time such as this.

Praise be to the God and Father of our Lord Jesus Christ, the Father of compassion and the God of all comfort, who comforts us in all our troubles, so that we can comfort those in any trouble with the comfort we ourselves receive from God.

–2 Corinthians 1:3–4 (NIV)

Life is short.

Even if we live to be one hundred years old, life is short. In church, we often sing the hymn "As a Life of a Flower," which depicts how our lives are like a flower. Flowers are beautiful, but they bloom only for a season. While breathtaking, the bloom dries up and falls off the plant.

In the book of James, he refers to our lives as a mist or a vapor that appears for a little while and then vanishes.

Selfishly, we want to see our children grow to become parents, and if we are lucky, to see them become grandparents, but our time on earth is as no time at all compared with the time we will spend in eternity.

Why, you do not even know what will happen tomorrow. What is your life? You are a mist that appears for a little while and then vanishes.

–James 4:14 (NIV)

Share in joy and in grief.

It is human nature to feel jealous when you see another woman who is pregnant or one who just welcomed a healthy baby home. Even though that is natural, it is not how Jesus wants us to feel or act. In the book of Romans, Paul tells us to mourn with those who mourn and rejoice with those who rejoice. You will be called upon to share the joy with the woman who has been given the gift of a baby. You will also be called upon to mourn and comfort families who share similar stories as yours.

Rejoice with those who rejoice; mourn with those who mourn.

—Romans 12:15 (NIV)

We have hope.

While there is a time to grieve, we should not grieve as if there is no hope of seeing our babies again. We will see them. In fact, we are told we will meet the Lord in the sky. Jesus will come down from heaven and those who have died will rise first, then those still living will meet them in the clouds.

In the book of 1 Corinthians 15, the Bible tells us that when Jesus returns, we will be changed in an instant. We will give up these frail bodies and exchange mortality for immortality.

For the Lord himself will come down from heaven, with a loud command, with the voice of the archangel and with the trumpet call of God, and the dead in Christ will rise first. After that, we who are still alive and are left will be caught up together with them in the clouds to meet the Lord in the air. And so we will be with the Lord forever.

—1 Thessalonians 4:1-17 (NIV)

There is a time for everything.

The book of Ecclesiastes tells us that there is a time for everything and a season for every purpose under the heavens. Life has seasons. Embrace the seasons—whatever season you are in—and help others in their season.

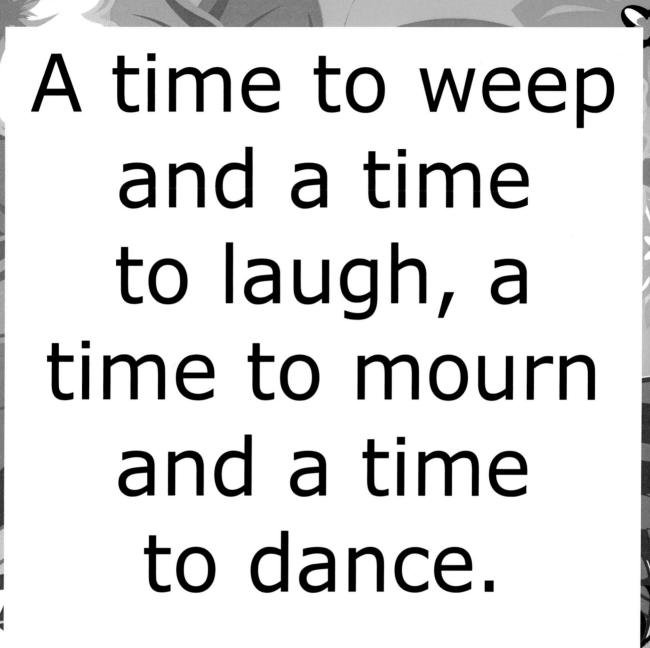

A time to weep and a time to laugh, a time to mourn and a time to dance.

—Ecclesiastes 3:4 (NIV)

Our babies are a perfect gift.

While losing a baby is beyond painful and devastating to families, a baby is still a glorious gift from God. While heartbreaking, the loss of my baby brought me closer to God. I felt like I had two choices in the days after loss: to blame Him or seek Him. Since then, my faith has grown. In this, my relationship with my family gained strength and substance with time. We no longer take life for granted.

Every good and
perfect gift is
from above,
coming down
from the Father
of the heavenly
lights, who does
not change like
shifting shadows.

—James 1:17 (NIV)

Have faith.

Always have faith. God is good. With faith, anything is possible. Sarah longed for a child. She faced infertility issues. Even though she was past the age for childbearing, God fulfilled His promise to her through her faith.

Whether you are also facing infertility or the loss of a child, have faith in your creator. Anything is possible with God.

And by faith even Sarah, who was past childbearing age, was enabled to bear children because she considered him faithful who had made the promise.

—Hebrews 11:11 (NIV)

Pray constantly.

The story of Hannah moves me. It is a beautiful story of prayer and a vow to the Lord. Hannah also faced infertility issues. Another woman taunted and provoked her because of her inability to conceive a child. Hannah prayed out of her great anguish and grief. The Lord answered her prayers, and she conceived a son. She devoted him to the Lord and glorified Him.

Pray earnestly for the baby you long to have. Pray for the child you were blessed to bring into this world. Pray for the unborn in our nation. Pray for the children in your extended family. Pray for the children in your community. Pray for the childcare workers, the school administrators, and the child advocates who protect our children. Never stop praying.

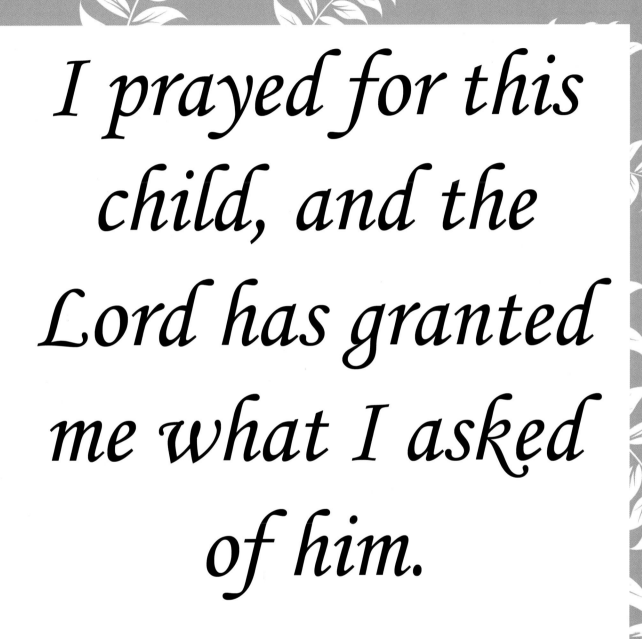

I prayed for this child, and the Lord has granted me what I asked of him.

–1 Samuel 1:27 (NIV)

God gave up His only Son.

You may have had to give a baby back to the Lord through miscarriage, stillbirth, infant loss, or the death of your grown child.

God also gave up His only Son for the sins of the world as the perfect sacrifice so that we can spend eternity with Him and our loved ones who died in Christ.

I hope this book brings you comfort and hope for the future. May God bless you and keep you.

For God so loved the world that he gave his one and only Son, that whoever believes in him shall not perish but have eternal life.

—John 3:16 (NIV)

Printed in the United States
by Baker & Taylor Publisher Services